■SCHOLASTIC

W9-AWG-762

Art Projects from Around the World

Grades 4–6

by Linda Evans, Karen Backus, and Mary Thompson

NEW YORK • TORONTO • LONDON • AUCKLAND • SYDNEY
MEXICO CITY • NEW DELHI • HONG KONG • BUENOS AIRES

Teaching *Resources*

This book is dedicated to artists from around
the world whose creativity and skills have inspired us
to share art from other cultures with our students.

Project introductions edited by Shoshana Wolfe
Cover design by Jason Robinson
Cover and interior photography by Studio 10
Interior illustrations by Cary Pillo
Interior design by Sydney Wright

ISBN: 0-439-38532-6
Copyright © 2006 by Linda Evans, Karen Backus, and Mary Thompson
Published by Scholastic Inc.
All rights reserved.
Printed in the U.S.A.

1 2 3 4 5 6 7 8 9 10   40   13 12 11 10 09 08 07 06

Contents

Introduction

Take a trip around the world with 20 unique art projects that connect to different countries! Some of the projects are based on an art form or craft from a particular culture. Other projects are inspired by a country's geography, history, or culture. You'll find paper fish kites from Japan, Carnival masks from the Caribbean, paper adinkra cloth from Ghana, and much more. The projects are designed to tie in to your curriculum and help students meet the social studies, geography, and visual arts standards.

The projects in this book are easy to create and use readily accessible materials. Each project includes:

◆ background information explaining how the project connects to the country of origin.

◆ illustrated, step-by-step directions.

◆ a materials list.

◆ recommended resources, such as books and Web sites.

◆ color photo of a sample project (see insert).

Creating multicultural art projects provides a hands-on way for students to learn about countries around the world as well as develop an appreciation of and respect for different cultures. We hope you and your students enjoy the journey!

Connections to the Standards

The activities in this book connect to the following standards and benchmarks outlined by Mid-continent Research for Education and Learning (McREL), a nationally recognized nonprofit organization that collects and synthesizes national and state K–12 standards.

Social Studies

—Understands various meanings of social group, general implications of group membership, and different ways that groups function:
  • Knows that language, stories, folktales, music, and artistic creations are expressions of culture

—Understands the folklore and other cultural contributions from various regions of the United States and how they helped to form a national heritage:
  • Understands how arts, crafts, music, and language of people from a variety of regions influenced the nation

—Understands selected attributes and historical developments of societies in Africa, the Americas, Asia, and Europe:
  • Understands the daily life, history, and beliefs of a country as reflected in dance, music, or other art forms (such as paintings, sculptures, and masks)

Geography

—Understands the characteristics and uses of maps, globes, and other geographic tools and techniques

—Knows the location of places, geographic features, and patterns of the environment

—Understands the characteristics and uses of spatial organization of Earth's surface

—Understands the physical and human characteristics of place

—Understands concepts of region

—Understands the nature and complexity of Earth's cultural mosaics

Visual Arts

—Understands and applies media, techniques, and processes related to the visual arts

—Knows how to use structures (e.g., sensory qualities, organizational principles, expressive features) and functions of art

—Knows a range of subject matter, symbols, and potential ideas in the visual arts

—Understands the characteristics and merits of one's own artwork and the artwork of others

—Understands the visual arts in relation to history and cultures:
  • Knows that the visual arts have both a history and a specific relationship to various cultures
  • Identifies specific works of art as belonging to particular cultures, times, and places
  • Knows how history, culture, and the visual arts can influence each other

—Understands similarities and differences among the characteristics of artworks from various eras and cultures (e.g., materials; visual, spatial, and temporal structures)

—Understands the historical and cultural contexts of a variety of art objects

—Understands how factors of time and place (e.g., climate, resources, ideas, technology) influence visual, spatial, or temporal characteristics that give meaning or function to a work of art

Source: Content Knowledge: A Compendium of Standards and Benchmarks for K–12 Education, 4th Edition (Mid-continent Research for Education and Learning, 2006).

⁘ How to Use This Book ⁘

The projects in this book are designed for flexible use. You can connect projects to topics in your social studies curriculum or use them on their own. Below are suggestions for making the most out of the learning experience.

Preparation

◆ In advance, review the background information and find photographs for students to use as reference or for inspiration. (Recommended resources are provided on the project pages.)

◆ Review the instructions, and create a sample project to show students.

◆ Gather the materials, and cut paper or other supplies to the size specified for the activity.

◆ Prepare the work space. For projects that involve painting or messy materials, cover tables with newspaper and have students wear smocks.

Introducing the Project

◆ Before students begin a project, point out the country on a map and present students with information about the country.

◆ Describe the project and explain how the project connects to the culture of that country. You'll find background information and recommended resources on each project page.

◆ Show students photographs that connect to the project. Look for examples in books, magazine articles, travel brochures, and online. Museum Web sites are an excellent source of quality images. If a project is based on a form of art, show photographs of the art form or bring in samples, if possible.

Cultural Sensitivity Note
Some of the projects in this book connect to topics with deep spiritual significance for native cultures. Please impress upon your students that these projects are intended to help them learn about these cultures and develop respect and appreciation for them.

Celebrate Cultures!

Here are additional ideas to immerse students in cultural studies:

* Create a bulletin board with maps, photos, postcards, travel brochures, and other information about a particular country.

* Play music from a particular country while students work on their projects.

* Invite people from different countries (or people who have traveled to different countries) to your classroom to share information and photos with students.

* Have students share information about their own heritage. Encourage them to talk to family members about where they or their ancestors are from.

* Plan a trip to a local museum so that students can view authentic cultural artwork.

* Have students research different aspects of the countries you have studied, such as arts and crafts, geography, history, and cultural groups.

Art Tips

* If a project involves painting or glue, plan in advance where you will place the projects to dry.

* If students are eager to begin before you have finished giving directions, distribute the art supplies after you have explained each step.

* Put tempera paint on foam trays or paper plates for easy cleanup.

* To clean tempera paint off paintbrushes, soak the brushes for ten minutes in water with a little dishwashing soap. The paint will rinse off quickly.

Display Tips

* For a simple way to mount a painting or drawing, give students sheets of paper that have been trimmed an inch on each side. For example, cut 12- by 18-inch paper so that it's 11 by 17 inches. You can then glue the painting or drawing onto a larger sheet of paper in a different color to create a border.

* To unify your displays, use large background paper or fabrics with cultural motifs that connect to the country of origin.

* In your displays, include information about the countries and the projects. Describe how the projects were created and how they connect to particular countries.

Korhogo Cloth Paintings

Students paint a design on fabric in the style of the Senufo people of Korhogo in West Africa.

The Senufo people of Ivory Coast have long cultivated cotton. Their centuries-old tradition of making "mud cloth" from the cotton began as a way of providing clothing for hunters. The deep, earthy colors of these handmade fabrics blend in with the landscape, providing hunters with effective camouflage. Because of its beauty and utility, however, the cloth is now widely used by nonhunters, too.

The process of making mud cloth can take two to three weeks. Senufo weavers weave cotton strips and then sew the strips together to make larger pieces of cloth. The cloth is soaked in a bath of water and cengura tree leaves, a mixture that prepares it for dyeing and also turns it a yellow-green. The cloth is then painted (traditionally, by women) with iron-rich mud, tree juices, and teas that range from tan to brown to black. After the paint has dried, the fabric is again soaked with leaves that deepen the colors. As a final step, some artisans bleach the unpainted areas to achieve a high-contrast effect. The bold designs include geometric patterns, scenes of village life, and animals and flowers. Some images are used to tell a story; others are believed to offer protection or good luck.

Getting Started

Place newspaper on tables and prepare the work space for painting. Have students wear smocks for this project. Point out Ivory Coast on a map and review the above information with students. If possible, bring in a sample of Korhogo cloth or show students photographs of it. Explain that they will be creating their own version of Korhogo cloth using watercolor paints and markers. Demonstrate the steps as students follow along.

Materials

- photographs of Korhogo cloth
- 12- by 10-inch canvas or other cotton cloth
- scrap paper
- pencils
- rulers
- black permanent markers (for use in a well-ventilated area)
- watercolor paints (brown, black, yellow, gray, and red)
- watercolor paintbrushes
- water containers

Resources

For Teachers

African Fabrics: Sewing Contemporary Fashion With Ethnic Flair by Ronke Luke-Boone (Krause, 2001). Provides background information on several traditional African textiles, including Korhogo cloth, as well as sewing projects that use these materials.

These Web sites provide photos of Korhogo cloth.

Library of Congress, Africana Collections
http://www.loc.gov/rr/amed/guide/afr-creative.html
Includes brief information.

Miami University Art Museum
http://www.fna.muohio.edu/amu/full/rug1.htm

Queens Library
http://www.queenslibrary.org/gallery/african/mudcloth.asp
Includes brief information.

Directions

1 On scrap paper, plan a design based on traditional designs found on Korhogo cloth. Draw an abstract form of an animal or person. Draw only a simple outline, leaving the inside of the figure blank.

2 With a pencil, draw a border around the piece of fabric. Use a ruler as needed to make the border even and straight. Then use a pencil to draw the outline of the figure in the center of the fabric.

3 Using black permanent marker, trace over the lines. Add line designs inside the sections within the figure.

4 Use watercolor paints to add color areas around the design. Lay flat to dry.

5 When the fabric is dry, pull loose the threads on the four edges to create a 1/4-inch fringe.

More Ideas

Have students research other textile designs from Africa, such as kente cloth (woven designs), adire cloth (designs created with wax resist), and adinkra cloth (stamped designs). Or have them explore textile designs from Indonesian, Indian, and Native American cultures. What is the function of these textiles? What can we learn about these cultures from their textiles?

Adinkra Cloth Prints

Students stamp colorful designs to create a paper representation of a traditional cloth from Ghana.

I n Ghana, West Africa, villagers work together to make adinkra cloth, which features colorful designs stamped onto fabric. Imported cloth is torn into strips and, traditionally, dyed one of several intense colors ranging from yellow to reddish brown to indigo. Once dry, the strips are sewn together. Meanwhile, tree bark is pounded and boiled to make printing dye. A grid of squares is drawn onto each piece of cloth and then stamps are used to apply the dye, filling the squares with printed designs. The stamps, carved from calabash gourds, contain symbols and patterns that communicate meanings and messages (see examples on page 11). *Adinkra* means "goodbye" in the Asante language. Traditionally, adinkra cloth was created using a dark-colored fabric and was worn during funeral ceremonies. In contemporary Ghana, the cloth is worn for many different occasions and celebrations and is available in brightly colored fabrics as well.

Materials

- photographs or samples of adinkra cloth
- adinkra symbols page (page 11)
- clean Styrofoam trays cut into 2-inch squares (4 per student)
- black fine-point markers
- scissors
- 2 1/2-inch cardboard squares
- 4- by 6-inch white paper (4 per student)
- water-based markers
- 12- by 18-inch construction paper (various colors)

Getting Started

Point out Ghana on a map and review the above information with students. If possible, bring in a sample of adinkra cloth or show students photographs of it. Explain that they will be creating their own representation of adinkra cloth with paper. Demonstrate the steps as students follow along.

TIPS

● If a symbol is difficult to cut out, cut closely around the shape. Then use a dull pencil to imprint the area around the shape.

● Nonsymmetrical symbols will print in reverse. When creating the stamp, reverse the image on the stamp so that it prints correctly.

● If ink seeps into the imprinted areas on the stamps, use a dull pencil to imprint those areas again.

Resources

For Teachers

African Textiles by John Gillow (Chronicle, 2003). This survey of textiles from different parts of Africa features hundreds of color photographs and illustrations. Includes information on adinkra cloth.

These Web sites provide photos of and information about adinkra cloth:

Library of Congress, Africana Collections
http://www.loc.gov/rr/amed/guide/afr-creative.html

National Museum of African Art
http://africa.si.edu/collections/advanpg.asp
To locate the information, set the search engine to find costumes and textiles from Ghana.

Directions

1 Select one of the symbols from page 11 or another reference. Using a marker, draw the symbol on a piece of foam. Carefully cut out the symbol. Use a dull pencil to imprint any areas in the center. Glue the symbol onto the cardboard square. Create four different stamps in this way (or have students share stamps).

2 Give each student four sheets of 4- by 6-inch white paper. Using a water-based marker, color the surface of the foam stamp. Print the symbols onto the paper, using different colors. Fill each sheet of paper with one symbol, or use a variety of symbols on each sheet.

3 Glue the four pages of printed designs onto a sheet of 12- by 18-inch construction paper, leaving equal space between the printed pages. Draw line designs on the construction paper around the printed pages.

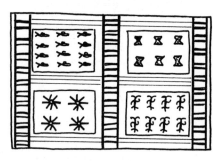

More Ideas

Have students research other African textiles, such as kente cloth and Korhogo cloth. Compare these textiles with adinkra cloth. Encourage students to observe fabric patterns in catalogs and magazines. Invite them to cut out samples of different patterned fabrics and create a collage with them.

Adinkra Symbols

Moon—Patience	King	Strength
Heart—Goodwill, Patience	Ram's Horns—Strength	Moon and Star—Faithfulness
Hen's Leg—Parental Care and Protection	Fern—Defiance	Agreement
Drum—Goodwill	Sanctity and Good Luck	Harmony

Seed Masks

Students use seeds and beans to create a mask inspired by traditional masks of the Democratic Republic of the Congo.

Wooden masks created by African carvers portray spirit beings, departed ancestors, and forces that control the social or natural world. Often combining human and animal features, these masks are crafted in a range of forms, covering only some of the wearer's features or the whole head, or combined with costumes to cover the entire body. The wearer of a mask, a trained male performer, is transformed by the mask and believed to conjure or create, rather than represent, the spirit or power the mask symbolizes. Masks are essential elements of ceremonies that also include music and dance.

The Kuba people of the south central region of the Democratic Republic of the Congo produce a variety of beautifully crafted objects carved from wood and decorated with paint, shells, and beads. As artisans, they are best known for masks representing three important ancestors and spirit beings—*Mwaash aMbooy*, a great king; *Ngady aMwaash*, his sister; and *Bwoom*, his brother. Lines from the eyes of female masks, including those that represent Ngady aMwaash, represent tears.

Materials

- photographs of masks from the Democratic Republic of the Congo
- 9- by 12-inch heavy tagboard
- pencils
- scissors
- craft knife (for adult use only)
- stapler
- tape
- black tempera paint
- easel brushes
- water containers
- variety of beans and seeds in several colors
- small containers
- nontoxic tacky glue
- 12- by 18-inch red construction paper (optional, for mounting)

Sensitivity Note

This project connects to a topic that holds deep spiritual significance for native cultures. Please impress upon your students that the project is intended to help them learn about these cultures and develop respect and appreciation for them.

Getting Started

Place newspaper on tables and prepare the work space for painting. Have students wear smocks for this project. Point out the Democratic Republic of the Congo on a map and review the above information with students. Show them photographs of masks from this country. Note the designs and materials used, such as shells and beads, to produce the patterns on the masks. Demonstrate the steps as students follow along.

Directions

1. Fold the tagboard in half lengthwise. Draw the outside edge of the mask and cut it out. (By keeping the tagboard folded, you will create a symmetrical mask.)

2. Draw an eye and cut it out. Trace the eye shape, and cut it out. (An adult should use a craft knife to cut out the eyes.)

3. Cut a 2-inch slit along the fold at the top of the mask. Overlap the slit edges and staple them together to form a three-dimensional mask. Repeat at the bottom of the mask. Place tape over staples on the back.

4. Draw a nose. Cut the bottom and sides of the nose and lift slightly. (An adult should use a craft knife or scissors to cut the nose.)

Resources

For Teachers

African Masks by Iris Hahner-Herzog (Prestel, 1998). Includes essays and nearly 250 photos of African masks found in the Barbier-Mueller Collection.

The Art of African Masks: Exploring Cultural Traditions by Carol Finley (Lerner, 1999). Explores the traditional use of African masks, how they are made, and the significance of their creation to the cultures in which they were developed. Appropriate for older students.

These Web sites provide photos of masks from the Democratic Republic of Congo:

Art Institute of Chicago
http://www.artic.edu/aic/collections/afr/highlight_item.php?acc=1982.1505
Mask of Ngady aMwaash

Virginia Museum of Fine Arts
http://www.vmfa.state.va.us/collections/77_13.html
Mask of Bwoom

5 Paint the mask with black tempera paint. Let dry.

6 Divide the class into groups. Distribute small containers of seeds and beans to each group. Instruct students to glue the seeds and beans in rows on the mask, keeping the design symmetrical on both sides. Encourage them to create patterns with the colors. For symmetry, use the same color seeds or beans on both sides of the mask.

7 Staple the finished mask to red paper for display (optional).

More Ideas

❖ Have students research the Kuba and other peoples of the Democratic Republic of the Congo.

❖ Have students make bracelets using seeds, beans, or other natural items. Encourage them to create patterns with the colors and shapes.

Serengeti Silhouettes

Students create a paper silhouette of an animal from the Serengeti and mount it on a colorful pastel sunset.

Wildebeests, buffalo, giraffes, cheetahs, lions, zebras, antelopes, and elephants roam the vast grasslands and woodlands of Tanzania and Kenya. Tall grasses, thorny bushes, and scattered ebony and mahogany trees form an unforgettable landscape the Masai people call the Serengeti, "the place where the land goes on forever." Each year enormous herds of wildebeests, zebras, and gazelles, pursued by predators, make a spectacular circular migration from Tanzania to Kenya and back again, in search of water and grazing land. The Great Migration, arduous and dangerous for the animals, is also essential for the renewal of the land. Sunsets over the Serengeti create some of the most breathtaking tableaux of the natural world.

Getting Started

Have students wear smocks for this project. Point out the Serengeti on a map and review the above information with students. Explain that a silhouette is an outline filled in with black against a lighter background. Show students pictures of animals and landscapes from the Serengeti Plain. Invite them to imagine they are taking a photo safari there to capture the animals in their natural habitat. The sun is setting with warm and brilliant colors. Against the backdrop of the red and orange sky, they see the silhouette of animal—it could be a lion, cheetah, zebra, or any other animal that calls the Serengeti home. Demonstrate the steps as students follow along.

Materials

- photographs of the Serengeti, including animals and landscapes
- 10- by 16-inch white paper
- orange, yellow, and red chalk or pastels
- paper towels
- 12- by 18-inch black paper
- white pencils or crayons
- scissors
- glue
- 12- by 18-inch white paper

Resources

For Teachers

Serengeti National Park's Official Site
http://www.serengeti.org
Includes photos and information about the park and its wildlife.

Serengeti Natural Order on the African Plain by Mitsuaki Iwago (Chronicle Books, 1987). Extraordinary photographs chronicle a year on the plains of Serengeti National Park.

For Students

Serengeti Migration: Africa's Animals on the Move by Lisa Lindblad (Hyperion, 1994). Beautiful photographs show the annual migration of wildebeests and zebras in the Serengeti.

Serengeti Plain (Wonders of the World) by Terri Willis (Heinemann, 1994). Color photographs and easy-to-understand text describe the national park and its wildlife.

Directions

1 Position the 10- by 16-inch white paper either horizontally or vertically, depending on your composition. Starting at the top of the paper, use the sides of the chalk to stroke across the paper. Overlap different colors to create the look of a sunset.

2 Blend the colors with a paper towel to create a soft effect.

3 On the black paper, use white pencil or crayon to draw a detailed outline of an animal on the Serengeti Plain. Encourage students to include tall grass and a tree, or some other feature of the habitat. This outline will be the silhouette.

4 Carefully cut out the outline and glue it onto the colorful sunset paper. Glue the sunset paper onto the 12- by 18-inch paper to create a frame.

More Ideas

Display a map of Africa on a bulletin board, highlighting the Serengeti Plain. List animals that you might see there, and hang the list beside the map. Display students' Serengeti silhouettes around the map. Add the question "Can you identify these animals?" Invite students to guess which animal is depicted in each project. To extend your studies, share African folktales that take place in the savannah. Have students research the area to learn about its climate and geographical features.

Hieroglyphic Printing and Figure Drawing

Students make a hieroglyphic stamp and create a drawing of an Egyptian figure.

Ancient Egyptian artists painted without knowledge of shadowing or foreshortening techniques later used to create perspective and give painted figures a three-dimensional quality. They also portrayed the size of objects relative to their social importance. A pharaoh, for example, is always the largest figure in any composition, regardless of his actual height or the presence of large buildings or large animals in the painting. Ancient Egyptian art often depicts a person from a side view, with the torso and shoulders facing front. The head was painted in profile so that the nose, considered an important feature, could be clearly and attractively depicted. The eye, however, is drawn as seen from the front, to show its importance as well. Ancient artists painted on papyrus paper and enlarged their paintings by use of a grid when adapting them for tomb walls. Archaeologists have also discovered paintings and carvings on caves, coffin cases, and alabaster statues. Egyptian hieroglyphs, which represent spoken language, are a mixture of sound symbols and picture signs.

Materials

- photographs of Egyptian art featuring people and hieroglyphic symbols
- Egyptian hieroglyphs page (page 21)
- clean Styrofoam trays cut into 2-inch squares
- pencils (sharp and dull)
- scissors
- 2 1/2-inch cardboard squares
- white glue
- 9- by 12-inch construction paper (various light colors)
- rulers
- water-based markers
- paper towels
- 5- by 8-inch white drawing paper
- yellow or tan chalk
- fine-tipped black markers
- red, gold, and blue gel pens
- glue sticks

Getting Started

Point out Egypt on a map and review the information on page 17 with students. Show them photographs of Egyptian art and note the style of it. Distribute copies of page 21 and discuss the hieroglyphs. Demonstrate the steps as students follow along.

Directions

1 Choose a hieroglyph and use a marker to draw it on a Styrofoam square. Use a dull pencil to imprint any areas in the center.

2 Carefully cut out the foam symbol. Glue it onto a cardboard square. Note: As an alternative to cutting out the symbol, draw the hieroglyph and then press over the lines with a dull pencil to create an imprint.

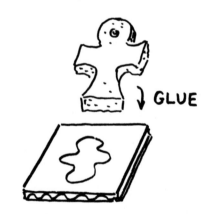

TIPS

- If a symbol is difficult to cut out, cut closely around the shape. Then use a dull pencil to imprint the area around the shape.

- Nonsymmetrical symbols will print in reverse. When creating the stamp, reverse the image on the stamp so that it prints correctly.

- If ink seeps into the imprinted areas on the stamps, use a dull pencil to imprint those areas again.

3 Choose a sheet of construction paper. Use a pencil and ruler to draw a two-inch border around the paper.

4 Using a marker, color the foam stamp and print along the border of the page. To change colors, rub the stamp with a damp paper towel and apply a new color. Use different stamps for variety, if desired. Encourage students to make their borders symmetrical. Let dry.

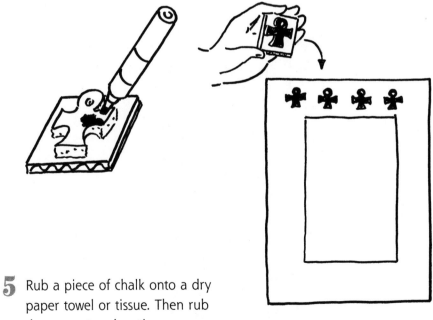

5 Rub a piece of chalk onto a dry paper towel or tissue. Then rub the paper towel or tissue over the sheet of white drawing paper.

Resources

For Teachers

The Art of Ancient Egypt by Gay Robbins (Harvard University Press, 2000). A comprehensive study of art in ancient Egypt.

How to Read Egyptian Hieroglyphics by Mark Collier and Bill Manley (University of California Press, 2003). A guide to reading hieroglyphics.

PBS: Egypt's Golden Empire http://www.pbs.org/empires/egypt Includes information about hieroglyphics and other aspects of life in ancient Egypt.

For Students

Ancient Egypt (DK Eyewitness Books) (DK, 2004). A beautifully illustrated classroom reference.

These Web sites provide information about hieroglyphics and other aspects of life in Ancient Egypt (preview the sites to determine if they are the appropriate reading level for your students):

Boston Museum of Fine Arts http://www.mfa.org/egypt/explore_ancient_egypt/index.html

The British Museum http://www.ancientegypt.co.uk/menu.html

NOVA Online Adventure http://www.pbs.org/wgbh/nova/pyramid/hieroglyph

6 Use fine-tipped markers to draw a simple symmetrical design around the border of the white paper.

7 In the center of the paper, draw an Egyptian figure in a profile stance. If desired, add hieroglyphs to the drawing. Use black marker to go over the lines of the drawing. Use gel pens to color small areas.

8 Glue the drawing to the center of the frame.

More Ideas

❖ Invite students to create a message with hieroglyphs.

❖ Have students research the discovery of King Tut's tomb in the Valley of the Kings.

❖ Have children try to stand in the profile stance characteristic of ancient Egyptian art.

Egyptian Hieroglyphs

Life	Eye of Horus	Fish	Vulture
Tree	Owl	Rope	Water
Bread	Flowers or Plants	Basket	Foot
Horned Viper	Pyramid	Weeping	City or Town

Elephant Boxes

Students make a simple box and decorate it with a design inspired by crafts of India.

A wealth of indigenous trees—walnut, teak, rosewood, sandalwood, bamboo, and ebony, among many others—has long provided Indian craftspeople with raw material and inspiration. Indian artisans create wooden boxes, bowls, utensils, toys, and furniture as well as elaborate works of art. They sculpt, carve, paint, wax, and lacquer wood, and create intricate inlaid designs with metals and contrasting woods. Ivory, the harvest of which is now outlawed in India, can be found inlaid on antique wooden pieces.

Elephants, a ubiquitous motif in Indian decorative arts, figure prominently in Indian mythology and represent strength and stability. A mother's dream of a white elephant heralded the birth of the Buddha; Ganesh, who has an elephant head and a human body, is a god adored and worshipped in the interest of fertility, prosperity, and well-being.

Getting Started

Photocopy the box template on medium-weight paper. If desired, enlarge the template. Point out India on a map and review the above information with students. Show them photographs of crafts from India, including small boxes inlaid with mosaics. Demonstrate the steps as students follow along.

Materials

- box template (page 24)
- 8¹/2- by 11-inch medium-weight paper (various light colors)
- scissors
- pencils
- colored markers, colored pencils, glitter pens, or gel markers
- glue stick and nontoxic tacky glue
- paper clips or clothespins
- small buttons, beads, rhinestones, or sequins (available in craft stores)

Directions

1 Carefully cut out the box template along the solid lines. (It is important to cut accurately to ensure success in constructing the box.)

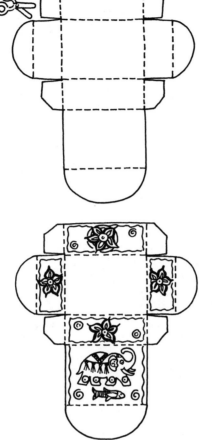

2 Show students which flaps will be the sides and top of the box. Use a pencil to draw designs on the sides and top of the box. Use markers or colored pencils to color the designs.

3 Fold the pattern along the dotted lines to construct the box. Use a small amount of glue on the side panels to secure them. Place a paper clip or clothespin on each side to hold the pieces in place while the glue dries.

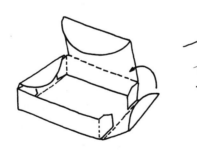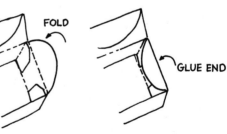

FOLD

GLUE END

4 Glue on a few sequins, buttons, beads, or small rhinestones to add texture and sparkle to the box.

More Ideas

◆ Learn about miniature paintings from India and other countries. Lacquer boxes with miniature paintings are also popular in Russia.

◆ Create other shapes and sizes of boxes.

Elephant Box Template

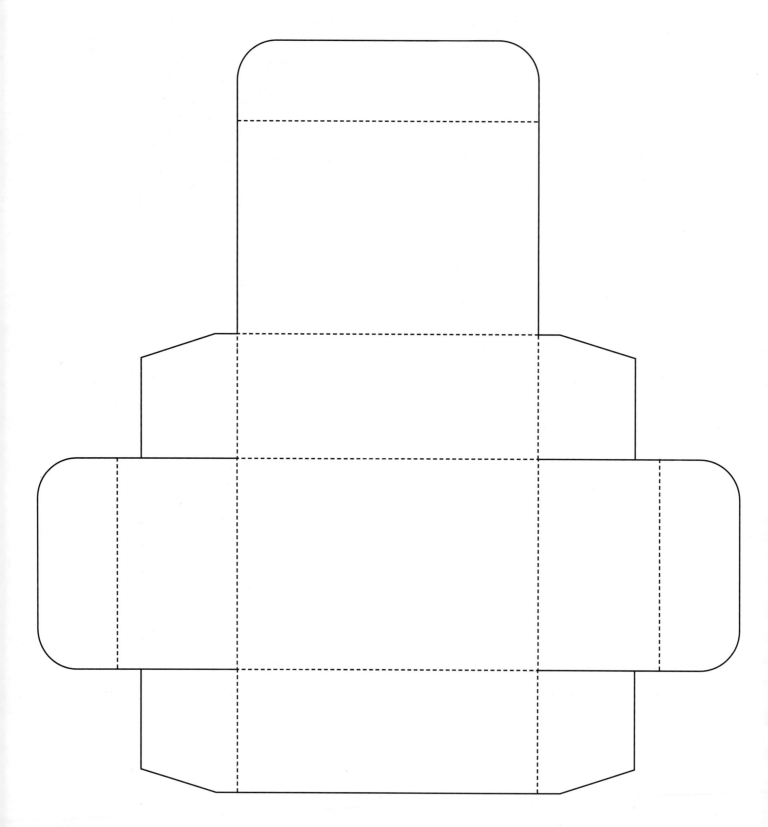

Art Projects From Around the World: Grades 4–6 Scholastic Teaching Resources

Hmong Story Cloth

Students use printmaking and fabric designs to create a story cloth in the style of the Hmong from southeastern Asia.

Hmong (pronounced "Mung") artisans sew beautiful designs on fabric, using appliqué, embroidery, batik, and cross-stitch. The *Pa Ndau*, or story cloth, is a traditional means of recording personal and cultural oral history. The designs incorporate elements of nature in the form of birds, fish, humans, trees, animals, plants, and crops. Traditionally, Pa Ndau were given as gifts to celebrate special occasions and were believed to offer love and protection to those who received them. Pa Ndau worn by babies, for example, disguised them as flowers and protected them from evil. It is their Pa Ndau that allow the Hmong to be recognized by ancestors in the afterlife, and then reincarnated as Hmong. Despite the development of a written language, contemporary Hmong continue to use this art form as a way of recording their personal histories and the story of their people.

Hmong means "free man," although the Hmong have suffered a brutal history and many forced relocations. Originally from Siberia and Central Asia, the Hmong have been forced by oppression, ethnic violence, and war into Myanmar, Vietnam, Thailand, and Laos. Many have immigrated to the United States; a large population now lives in the city of Fresno, California.

Materials

- photographs of Hmong designs and story cloth
- pencils
- sketch paper
- clean Styrofoam trays or foam board cut into 3-inch squares
- ballpoint pen
- 3½-inch cardboard square
- white glue
- water-based markers
- 12-inch white paper square
- paper towels
- 6-inch felt or fabric square
- scissors
- felt or fabric scraps

Getting Started

Point out Myanmar, Vietnam, Laos, and Cambodia and review the information on page 25 with students. Show students photographs of Hmong designs and story cloths. Have them refer to these photographs as they work on their projects. Demonstrate the steps as students follow along.

Directions

1 Sketch a design that you will use to print on the border of your project. Using a ballpoint pen, draw the design on the three-inch Styrofoam square. Press into the foam to create an imprint.

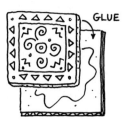

2 Glue the foam square onto a cardboard square.

3 Choose a marker and color the entire foam square. Press the foam square into the corner of the 12-inch paper to print. Continue printing by reapplying color each time before you print. To change colors, wipe the foam with a paper towel. Continue to print until the border is complete.

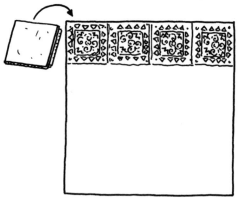

TIP

If ink seeps into the imprinted areas on the stamps, use a dull pencil to imprint those areas again.

4 Glue the six-inch fabric square to the center of the paper so that the border frames it.

5 Choose an image from nature to depict on the fabric. First, draw an outline of the image on scrap paper. Cut out the shape.

6 Trace the shape onto a piece of fabric and cut it out. Glue the shape onto the fabric square. Glue on additional fabric pieces to add details.

More Ideas

Compare and contrast symbols and traditions of Hmong textile designs with those of Native American or African cultures.

Resources

For Teachers

Hmong Textile Designs by Anthony Chan (Stemmer House, 1990). A reference of the designs and symbols in Hmong story cloths.

University of California, Irvine Libraries
http://www.lib.uci.edu/libraries/ collections/sea/hmong.html Includes information about Hmong textiles and photographs of samples.

For Students

Dia's Story Cloth by Dia Cha (Lee & Low Books, 1996). A story cloth chronicles the significant and traumatic events in the lives of the author and her family, as they move from Laos to a refugee camp in Thailand to the United States.

The Hmong of Southeast Asia (First Peoples) by Sandra Millet (Lerner, 2001). Photos and text describe different aspects of Hmong culture.

Nine-in-One Grr! Grr! A Folktale From the Hmong People of Laos by Blia Xiong and Cathy Spagnoli (Children's Book Press, 1989). Eu, a bird, saves civilization by tricking a tiger in this lively retelling of a traditional Hmong folktale.

Batik

Students design a piece of batik fabric, using a mixture of flour and water.

The ancient art of batik is a process that utilizes hot melted wax and dyes to create intricate designs on cotton fabric. Skilled artisans may spend weeks producing a single piece of fabric by traditional methods that involve hand-drawing designs with a wax-application tool called a *tjanting* (pronounced "chanting"), dipping the fabric in handmade dye, allowing it to dry, and then cracking and reapplying the wax and dipping the fabric in one or more new colors to create a multicolored design. The dyes soak into the fabric except where the wax has been applied, creating areas where the original white or cream color of the fabric is visible once the wax has been removed.

Traditionally, batik dyes were made from the leaves of the indigo plant and the bark of various trees. Both men and women wear batik material that has been fashioned into shawls, sarongs (a kind of skirt worn by both men and women), and head coverings.

While batiks produced by hand remain highly prized, advances in technology have made it possible to produce the fabric more quickly. A more modern method of applying wax to fabric involves the use of *tjaps* (pronounced "chops"), which are ribbons of copper formed into designs and soldered into blocks. The blocks are then dipped into hot wax and stamped onto fabric. A skilled artisan can reproduce the look of a hand-drawn batik pattern using this method.

Getting Started

In advance, whisk flour and water together until they form a thick paste, like a pudding. Whisk until the mixture has no lumps. Put a small amount in the containers and distribute to worktables for students to share. Each student will need a small amount of paste.

Materials

- photographs or samples of batik fabric (available at some fabric stores)
- flour
- water
- wire whisk
- small bowl
- small containers
- acrylic paints
- 9- by 12-inch white drawing paper
- pencils
- 9- by 12-inch unbleached muslin
- acrylic paintbrushes (fine-tipped, medium, and large)
- large container or sink
- iron (for adult use only)
- 11- by 14-inch dark-colored and black construction paper
- glue

Add water to dilute the acrylic paint to a watery consistency. The paint should be fluid enough to apply it smoothly to the muslin using a paintbrush. Test this out first. If the paint is too watery, add a bit more paint. If it is too thick, add a bit more water. Place newspaper on the tables and prepare the work space for painting. Have students wear smocks for this project.

Point out Indonesia on a map and review the information on page 28 with students. Show them photographs or samples of batik material. Point out the crackled effect in the pattern of the material, created by the dye seeping into the cracked wax during the dyeing process. Demonstrate the steps as students follow along.

Directions

1 Choose the subject matter for your design, such as flowers, fish, butterflies, or other creatures. Abstract or symmetrical designs work well. Using pencil, sketch the design on the white paper. Make sure to use a simple line design. Transfer the design onto the material, drawing lightly with a pencil.

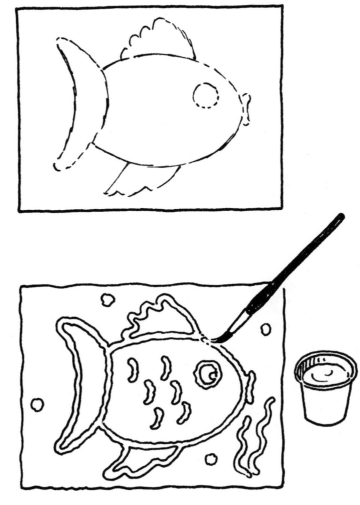

2 Use a fine-tipped paintbrush to apply the flour mixture to the design. Cover all lines of the design with a thin line of the flour mixture. Extra flour lines may be added around the design. (The flour mixture will prevent areas of the cloth from absorbing paint in later steps. These sections will remain white.) Set aside to dry.

Resources

For Teachers

Batik by Sarah Tucker (Trafalgar Square Press, 1999). Learn the art of batik following seven simple activities.

Batik: From the Courts of Java and Sumatra by Rudolf G. Smend (Periplus, 2004). A tour of Java includes a look into the various Asian influences on batik.

Creative Batik by Rosi Robinson (Search Press, 2001). Learn batik by following these simple instructions that are supplemented by photos.

3 When the flour mixture is dry, crack it slightly.

4 Use a medium or large paintbrush to paint over the entire cloth with diluted acrylic paint. The dry flour mixture lines will act as a resist, just as the wax does in the batik process. Let dry.

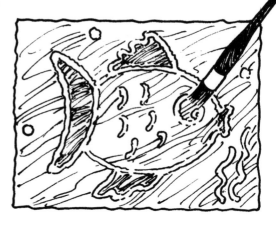

5 In the sink or a large container of warm water, gently wash off the flour mixture until the cloth is clean. The acrylic paint will have stained the material around the flour mixture.

More Ideas

◆ To display the batik, you might want to iron it first. (An adult should complete this step, supervising closely for safety. Do not leave the hot iron where students can access it.) Mount on colored construction paper that is positioned like a diamond. Glue a sheet of black paper behind it that is positioned like a square. (See photo.)

◆ Try the batik process on a T-shirt or larger piece of material. Make a cloth bag out of the batik fabric.

◆ Batik can also be done using wax candles. Rub the candle wax heavily over the drawn lines on the material. Crack the wax before painting. Paint as directed above. Remove the wax by placing a paper bag over the material and ironing until the wax is removed. (An adult should complete this step.)

Fish Kites

Students make and fly a tissue paper fish kite celebrating the Japanese tradition.

Each year on May 5, Japanese families fly kites in celebration of *Kodomo-no-hi*, or Boys' Day. *Koinobori*, colorful carp-shaped streamers, are displayed outside family homes during this 500-year-old festival, which coincides with the beginning of summer on the lunar calendar. Although the festival has come to be known as the Children's Festival, contemporary Japanese people continue to recognize the day as a special celebration of boyhood. (Girls' Day, though not a national holiday, is celebrated in March.) Families celebrating Kodomo-no-hi also display samurai dolls inside their homes and prepare special foods for the festival. Koinobori are fashioned after the carp, a fish that symbolizes courage, power, and determination because it swims against the current. The carp represents the strength and courage children will need in their own lives.

Getting Started

In advance, photocopy each half of the fish kite template (pages 34–35). Enlarge each half to fit an 11- by 17-inch sheet of paper. Tape the two pages together so that both sides of the template line up. Cut out the template.

Point out Japan on a map and review the above information with students. Show them photographs of Japanese kites. Demonstrate the steps as students follow along.

Materials

- photographs of Japanese kites and art
- fish kite template (pages 34–35)
- 14- by 20-inch colored tissue paper (2 sheets of the same color per student)
- stapler
- pencils
- scissors
- water-based markers
- 2- by 15-inch tissue paper strips (various colors)
- glue stick
- 1- by 9-inch oak tag strips
- hole punch
- 9-foot piece of lightweight string
- craft sticks

Directions

1. Staple together two pieces of tissue paper. Place the fish template on top of the tissue, and use a pencil to trace the template. Cut out the shape through both sheets so that you have two identical fish shapes.

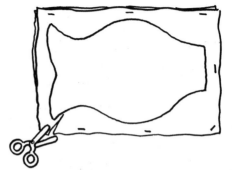

2. Place newspaper on the table. Using markers, draw scales, gills, an eye, and a tail on the tissue paper. Some water-based markers will bleed through the second layer. This makes it easier to create a backside that matches the front. Otherwise, draw details on both sides.

GLUE

3. Place one fish with the blank side facing up. Glue around the edges of the fish, making sure not to glue the mouth area. Gently place several streamers on top of the glued area. Place glue on top of the streamers.

4. With a partner, carefully lift the other fish and place it directly on top of the glued fish. Press to seal around all the edges except the mouth. (This is to avoid having air escape from the kite.)

(Activity continued on page 33.)

IVORY COAST
**Korhogo
Cloth Paintings**
page 7

GHANA
**Adinkra
Cloth
Prints**
page 9

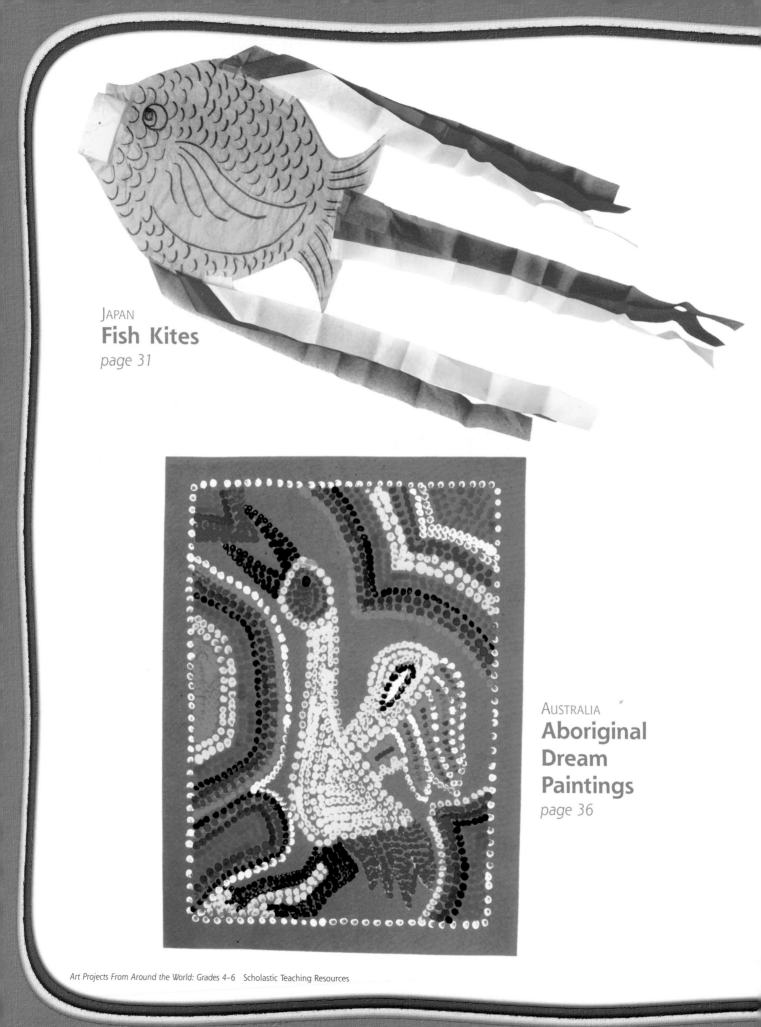

JAPAN
Fish Kites
page 31

AUSTRALIA
**Aboriginal
Dream
Paintings**
page 36

5 Hold the fish kite by the mouth opening. Place the oak tag strip inside the mouth. Cut so that it fits as a circle inside the mouth. Staple the ends of the strip together.

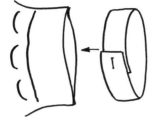

6 Fold the top edge of the tissue paper mouth over the oak tag. Staple securely, using eight to ten staples.

7 Use a hole punch to punch two holes opposite each other on the mouth.

8 Tie a piece of string through each hole. Tie the two pieces together as shown. Wrap the extra string around a craft stick for a handle. (Note: The tissue paper forms a kind of wind sock that fills out when the wind blows through it.)

TIE

More Ideas

❖ Fly the kite on a dry day so that the tissue paper does not get wet.

❖ Have students learn about and make other kinds of kites. Then compare how the different kites fly.

Resources

For Teachers

The Kite Making Handbook by Rossella Guerra and Giuseppe Ferlegna (David & Charles, 2004). This handbook reviews the basics of kite making.

Kites by David Pelham (Overlook, 2000). A guide to making and flying various types of kites.

For Students

Asian Kites by Wayne Hosking (Tuttle, 2005). Includes background information about kite making in Asia and 15 easy-to-make kites (seven of which are from Japan).

Shibumi and the Kitemaker by Mercer Mayer (Marshall Cavendish, 1999). In this picture book for younger students, the emperor's daughter insists on using a kite to fly above the poverty-stricken city until her father makes it as beautiful as his palace grounds.

Fish Kite Template

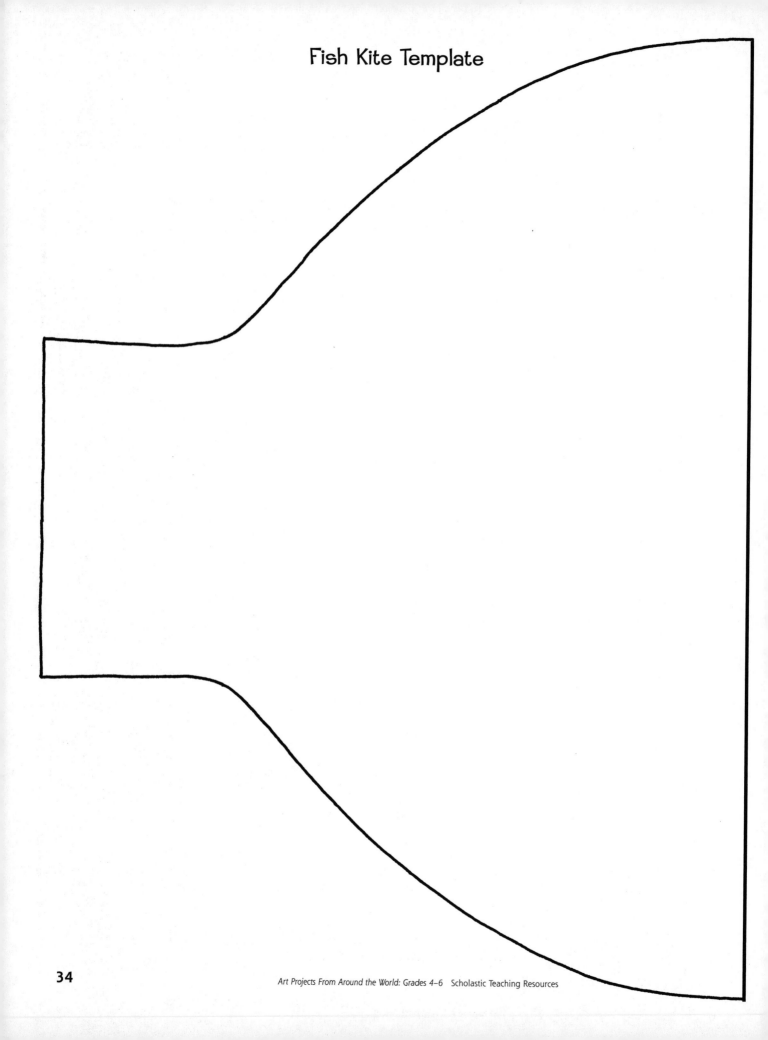

Art Projects From Around the World: Grades 4–6 Scholastic Teaching Resources

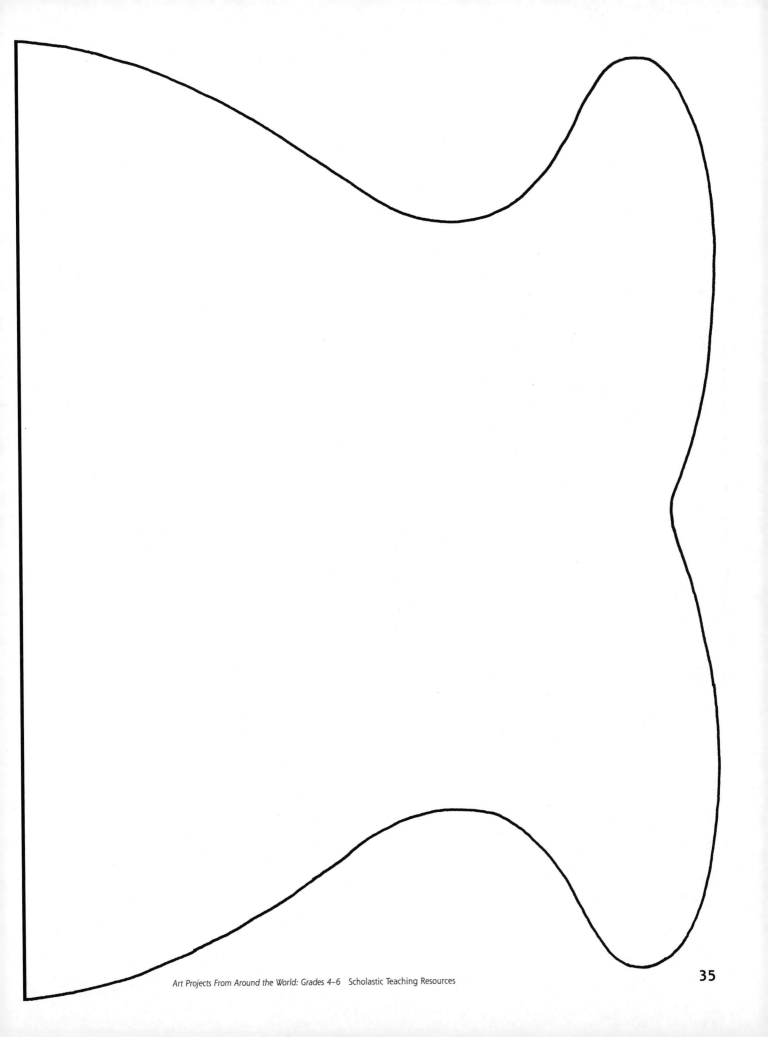

Aboriginal Dream Paintings

Students depict an animal in the colorful dot painting style of the Aborigines.

Archaeologists believe that the indigenous people of Australia, known as Aborigines, may have inhabited Australia and its islands for more than 60,000 years. The spiritual and religious beliefs of most contemporary Aborigines remain rooted in the traditions of their ancient culture, despite centuries of colonialism and contact with other peoples and traditions. Central to Aboriginal spirituality is the belief that ancestral beings created everything in the world during a time called Dreamtime, and that they remain part of our world—as rocks, hills, or stars, for example.

Aboriginal artists are guided in their work by a desire to be in touch with the Dreamtime. The sacred artifacts crafted by Aborigines for thousands of years—boomerangs, body decorations, wooden sculpture, bark paintings, and art made from rocks and sand—are produced for ceremonial purposes and, traditionally, destroyed afterward. Animals and figures are represented in their most basic, abstract forms, and each piece of art communicates a story, message, spiritual idea, or everyday happening. In recent decades Aboriginal artists have been encouraged to save their artwork, and it is now recognized by non-Aborigines as an important art form and displayed in museums and galleries throughout the world.

Getting Started

Place newspaper on tables and prepare the work space for painting. Have students wear smocks for this project. Point out Australia on a map and review the above information with them. Show students photographs of Aboriginal dream paintings, and note that animals are sometimes shown in them. Tell students that they will create a project that is inspired by the subject matter and style of Aboriginal dream paintings. Explain that these paintings hold deep meaning for Aborigines. Demonstrate the steps as students follow along.

Materials

- photographs of Aboriginal dream paintings and animals of Australia
- 12- by 18-inch paper
- pencils
- rulers
- colored pencils
- cotton swabs
- brown, white, black, red, and yellow tempera paint

Sensitivity Note

This project connects to a topic that holds spiritual significance for native cultures. Please impress upon your students that the project is intended to help them learn about these cultures and develop respect and appreciation for them.

Directions

1 Sketch a few animals from Australia in the abstract style of Aboriginal art. Determine which one you will use as the basis for your painting. Position the paper horizontally or vertically, depending upon your composition.

2 Use a ruler and a pencil to draw a border.

3 Using a pencil, draw the outline of your animal so that it fills the page. Refer to a photograph of the animal as needed.

4 Use colored pencils to add line designs and color certain areas. (Tip: High-quality colored pencils are softer and will produce a richer color.)

5 Using tempera paint, make a dot pattern with the cotton swabs. Paint a dot pattern along the border.

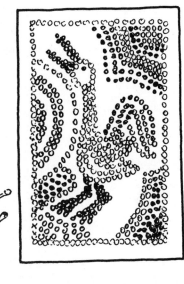

More Ideas

◆ Display the paintings along with facts about Aboriginal art and culture.

◆ Have students study other kinds of Aboriginal art, such as bark paintings, rock paintings, and carved emu eggs. Introduce them to the didgeridoo, a traditional Aboriginal instrument, and play a CD or audiocassette of music featuring this instrument.

Resources

For Teachers

Dreamings: The Art of Aboriginal Australia by Peter Sutton (George Braziller, 1997). This beautiful volume from the South Australia Museum and the Asia Society Galleries examines Aboriginal art and its connection to Dreamtime.

For Students

Aboriginal Art of Australia: Exploring Cultural Traditions by Carol Finley (Lerner, 1999). Explores Aboriginal art from several Australian regions.

The Kookabura and Other Stories (CD) by Dal Burns (Gifts From the Art, 2001). These seven stories, based on Aboriginal myths, complement studies of Aboriginal culture.

Celtic Letters

Students illustrate their initials in the style of Celtic lettering.

The Book of Kells is one of the most famous examples of an illuminated manuscript. Historians believe the 680-page manuscript was written and illustrated by Irish monks in the medieval era, around 800 A.D. Despite a harrowing theft by Vikings and the loss of its cover, most of the manuscript is still intact and is kept at the library of Trinity College in Dublin.

Medieval manuscripts were drawn on vellum, a thin layer of calfskin, and the breathtakingly detailed illustrations were painted in exotic yellow, red, indigo, black, and purple pigments. Intricate calligraphy, swirling shapes, and elaborate Celtic knots and mazes adorn the pages of the Book of Kells. Large initial letters are decorated with human forms and those of mice, cats, dogs, lions, snakes, eagles, ducks, otters, and birds. Animals in the illustrations often hold something in their mouths: intertwining vines, knots, or even other animals. In later years a thin layer of gold or silver leaf was added to designs in manuscripts from many parts of Europe. Although the term "illuminated manuscripts" originally applied only to these manuscripts, all illustrated manuscripts from the Middle Ages and Renaissance are commonly referred to as illuminated.

Getting Started

Place newspaper on tables and prepare the work space for painting. Have students wear smocks for this project. Point out Ireland on a map and review the above information with students. Show them photographs of illuminated letters and distribute copies of page 40. Demonstrate the steps as students follow along.

Directions

1 Tear along the edges of the tracing paper to give it an antique look. Use a large brush to paint the entire surface of the paper. Use a combination of orange and brown paint with a lot of water to create an antique look. Let dry on paper towels.

Materials

- photographs or samples of illuminated letters
- Celtic letters sheet (page 40)
- 7- by 10-inch tracing paper
- watercolor paints
- paintbrushes (various sizes)
- water containers
- paper towels
- 7- by 10-inch drawing paper
- pencils
- coins or small chips (for tracing)
- black fine-point markers
- fine-point markers or colored pencils
- 9- by 12-inch colored construction paper
- glue

2 On the drawing paper, draw your first initial in a Celtic style of lettering. Draw a large outline of the letter to create an area inside the letter.

3 Inside the letter, draw designs inspired by Celtic lettering. Include swirls, knots, or animals. Vines and graceful swirls work well, flowing inside and outside of the letter. To draw small circles, trace coins. Draw designs inside the circles.

4 Place the tracing paper on top of the completed letter. Trace the letter with a black fine-point marker.

5 Color the inside of the designs, using fine-point markers, colored pencils, or a fine-tipped brush and watercolor paints.

6 Mount on colored construction paper.

More Ideas

Have students study other styles of lettering. Invite them to illustrate a favorite quotation or a verse of a song in calligraphy.

Resources

For Teachers

The Book of Kells: An Illustrated Introduction by Bernard Meehan (Thames & Hudson, 1994). Includes more than 100 color illustrations of pages from the Book of Kells.

A Celtic Alphabet by Andrew Whitson (Appletree Press, 1997). Features an illuminated alphabet based on the Book of Kells as well as other sources.

Draw Your Own Celtic Designs by David James (Davis & Charles, 2003). This guide to creating your own Celtic designs includes information on Celtic art and a section covering Celtic lettering.

The Illuminated Alphabet by Timothy Noad, Patricia Seligman (Sterling, 1994). The Celtic alphabet is just one showcased in this beautiful volume.

For Students

The Celts (See Through History) by Hazel Mary Martell (Viking, 1995). Informative text, photographs, and drawings provide a detailed account of the life and history of the Celtic people. Students will enjoy lifting transparent overlays to discover interior scenes of buildings and structures.

Celtic Letters

Art Projects From Around the World: Grades 4–6 Scholastic Teaching Resources

Stained Glass Windows

Students create a colorful project that resembles stained glass.

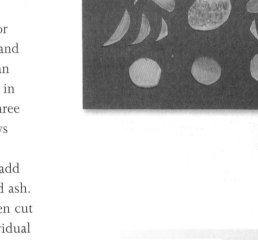

During the medieval period, artists created dazzling stained glass windows for the great churches and cathedrals of Europe. As they have done for centuries, rays from the sun still pass through the glass and illuminate these vast spaces with colored light. More than one hundred large stained glass windows were installed in the Gothic Chartres Cathedral in France in the 1200s. Three of these are magnificent rose windows, circular windows with glass placed in a geometric, roselike pattern.

To create intricate stained glass images, artisans add powdered metals to a molten mixture of sand and wood ash. Flattened or spun into sheets and cooled, the glass is then cut and arranged over a design drawn on a board. The individual pieces of glass are fitted together with strips of soft lead, which are soldered together to create a final design.

Getting Started

Point out France on a map and review the above information with students. Show them photographs of stained glass windows. Demonstrate the steps as students follow along.

Directions

1 Position the black paper vertically. Trim the top of the paper to form a Gothic-style arch.

Materials

- photographs of stained glass windows
- 9- by 12-inch black construction paper
- scissors
- white pencils
- dull pencils
- 9- by 12-inch sheets of acetate or Mylar (clear plastic)
- permanent markers (for use in a well-ventilated area)
- stapler

Resources

For Teachers

Medieval and Renaissance Stained Glass in the Victoria and Albert Museum by Paul Williamson (Victoria & Albert Museum, 2004). An overview of the museum's collection of stained glass, which includes works from France and other countries.

Stained Glass: From Its Origins to the Present by Virginia Chieffo Raquin (Harry N. Abrams, 2003). More than 500 color photographs enhance this survey of stained glass. Includes pieces from Chartres.

2 Plan a simple design of easy-to-cut shapes for your stained glass window. The shapes should take up no more than half the paper. Draw the shapes with white pencil.

3 To cut out the shapes, first poke a hole in the center with a dull pencil. Then insert the scissors and cut out the shape. The black paper in between the shapes will resemble the lead used to hold the window glass together.

4 Place the black paper on top of the acetate sheet. Trace around the top of the black paper. Cut the acetate sheet so that it matches the shape of the black paper. Staple the acetate sheet to the back of the black paper.

5 Use permanent marker to color the sections of acetate showing through the black paper.

More Ideas

❖ Hang the completed projects in a window so that light will shine through them.

❖ Have students research and compare the work of stained glass artists such as John LaFarge, Louis C. Tiffany, and William Morris.

Paper Cutting

Students create symmetrical paper designs inspired by the Polish art of paper cutting.

Wycinanki (vee-chee-nahn-kee), paper cutting, is a popular craft in Poland, with roots in 19th-century culture. In those days Polish people living on farms used the tools available to them—sheep shears—to cut detailed designs from bark, leather, and colored paper to decorate their homes for Easter. Traditional designs often included lacelike symmetrical and repeating patterns and were inspired by common scenes of farm life. Trees of life, people in traditional dress, roosters, fruits, flowers, medallions, and religious symbols appear frequently in wycinanki.

As the art form developed, people began to layer different papers to make multicolored wycinanki, and distinctive designs began to evolve in different regions of Poland. Wycinanki are now created for other holidays and for a variety of decorating purposes. Originally, the paper cuts were applied directly to whitewashed walls, but as the craft evolved, people began to use them to decorate a variety of household objects including furniture and window frames.

Getting Started

Point out Poland on a map and review the above information with students. Show them photographs of traditional Polish paper cutting. Demonstrate the steps as students follow along.

Directions

FOLD

1 Fold a sheet of black paper in half lengthwise or widthwise. Using white pencil or chalk, draw one half of the design on the folded page.

Materials

- photographs of Polish paper cutting
- 9- by 12-inch black, white, and colored construction paper
- white pencils or chalk
- scissors
- child-safe scissors with decorative edges (optional)
- glue sticks

Resources

For Teachers

Folk Art Designs From Polish Wycinanki and Swiss and German Scherenschnitte by Ramona Jablonski (Stemmer House, 1978). Features a section on Polish Wycinanki-based folk designs.

Polish Wycinanki Designs by Frances Drwal (Stemmer House, 1984). A guide to basic Polish paper cutting designs and techniques.

2 Continue to draw swirling lines, straight lines, or simple shapes such as birds or leaves on top of or in the design. Connect all the shapes so that the design can be cut in one piece.

3 Carefully cut along the lines of your design. As you unfold the paper, the design will be symmetrical. If desired, have students use child-safe scissors with a decorative edge.

4 Use a glue stick to mount the design on white or colored paper.

5 Use colored paper scraps to create small cutouts. Cut two of each shape. Glue them onto the design, maintaining symmetry. Layer the cutouts to create a visually interesting design.

More Ideas

◆ Research paper cutouts from other countries, such as China, Germany, and Spain.

◆ Cut paper chains to display with the finished projects.

Ancient Vase Paintings

Students illustrate a Greek myth or a scene from ancient Greek life on a paper vase.

A great deal of our knowledge of ancient Greece comes from detailed painting on pottery. Using a potter's wheel, ancient Greeks shaped clay into containers that were used to store and carry food and liquids. Historians believe that Athenian potters first decorated vessels using a black-figure technique: Artisans painted designs with a slip (liquid clay) that turned black during firing and contrasted with the natural red color of the clay. The potter Andokides is believed to have invented a red-figure technique in the mid-sixth century B.C., in which the background is painted with the slip and the figures remain the color of the clay. The red-figure technique allowed artisans to produce detailed figures without adding pigments or using a sharp tool to incise, or etch, the slip.

Illustrations on the earliest pots depict Greek gods and goddesses and scenes of war. Later works provide images of athletic competition, domestic life, and wedding preparations.

Getting Started

Have students wear smocks for this project. Point out Greece on a map and review the above information with students. Show them photographs of ancient Greek vases as well as motifs (patterns) in ancient Greek art. Distribute copies of page 47. Demonstrate the steps as students follow along.

Materials

- photographs of Greek vases
- Greek vase shapes and motifs page (page 47)
- 12- by 18-inch thin white drawing paper
- pencils
- black markers
- colored chalk or pastels
- paper towels
- scissors
- glue or glue sticks
- 12- by 18-inch black paper

Resources

For Teachers

These Web sites provide photographs and information about ancient Greek vases.

The Metropolitan Museum of Art
http://www.metmuseum.org/toah/hd/evdy/hd_evdy.htm

Tufts University: The Perseus Digital Library
http://www.perseus.tufts.edu/cgi-bin/browser?object=Vase&field=Keyword
Features a searchable database of images.

University of Pennsylvania Museum of Archaeology and Anthropology
http://www.museum.upenn.edu/Greek_World/pottery.html

For Students

Ancient Greece (DK Eyewitness Books) (DK, 2004). Packed with illustrations, this visually appealing resource describes daily life in ancient Greece and includes information on Greek myths and art.

Ancient Greek Art by Susie Hodge (Heinemann, 1998). A short but informative overview of different forms of ancient Greek art, including pottery.

The British Museum
http://www.ancientgreece.co.uk/menu.html
Includes information on life in Ancient Greece.

Directions

1 Fold the white paper in half lengthwise. Use a pencil to draw one half of a Greek vase on the folded page. Curve the top and bottom of the vase so that it looks round.

2 While the paper is still folded, draw Greek-inspired patterns, such as wavy or zigzag lines, triangles, and squares, on half of the vase. Draw heavily so that the design will show through the folded paper.

3 Turn over the paper, keeping it folded. Trace the lines showing through the page. When you open the page, the designs will be symmetrical.

4 Open the page. In the center of the vase, illustrate a myth, everyday activity, or sporting event from ancient Greece. If illustrating people, show them in profile. Refer to samples of ancient Greek art as you draw.

5 Use a black marker to trace over the drawing and fill in details.

6 Select chalks that suggest a terra-cotta color. Gently use the sides of the chalk to color the vase. To achieve a 3-D effect, color the sides darker. Blend the colors with a paper towel.

7 Cut out the vase and glue it onto black paper.

More Ideas

❖ Read ancient Greek myths and have students illustrate them.

❖ Compare ancient Greek illustrations of the first Olympics to photographs of modern-day Olympics.

Greek Vase Shapes and Motifs

Amphora

Calyx-Krater

Hydria

Ornate Architecture Designs

Students design a Russian-style building, using colored pencils.

The magnificent St. Basil's Cathedral has fascinated visitors to St. Petersburg's Red Square since its construction in the mid-16th century. Built to celebrate the Russian victory over the Tartars, the church consists of eight individual structures, each with its own distinctly patterned onion dome or cupola and numerous arches, towers, and spires. The overall effect is stunning. Ivan the Terrible, a notorious ruler, was the commissioner of the cathedral.

Getting Started

Point out Russia on a map and review the above information with students. Show them photographs of the Russian onion-dome style of architecture, such as St. Basil's Cathedral in St. Petersburg's Red Square. Note the features of this style, such as the pointed tops of the domes and the towers beneath. Demonstrate the steps as students follow along.

Directions

1 Sketch several fanciful buildings that feature the onion-dome style of architecture. Have students refer to photographs as they draw. Choose the sketch that you will use as the basis for your drawing.

Materials

- photographs of Russian onion-dome architecture, such as St. Basil's Cathedral
- sketch paper
- pencils
- 18- by 24-inch sulfite-based construction paper in dark colors such as blue, black, purple, and green
- colored pencils (including white)
- 2- by 22-inch white construction paper (2 per student)
- 2- by 12-inch strips white construction paper (2 per student)
- decorative rubber stamps that will fit on the white strips
- ink pads or water-based markers
- damp paper towels
- glue

2 Using a white pencil on dark-colored paper, draw overlapping buildings on the page. Add details to the buildings, such as arches, doors, spires, and windows. Leave a blank border around the page.

3 Use colored pencils to decorate the buildings. Draw motif patterns on the buildings and domes. Gold and silver pencils add a decorative touch. Press firmly so that the colors stand out against the background paper.

4 Use rubber stamps and ink pads to create a border design on the white paper strips. If using water-based markers, color the stamp and immediately press it onto the paper strip. To change colors, rub the stamp with a damp paper towel, and color it again. Create matching patterns on the two long strips (for the top and bottom borders) and the two shorter strips (for the side borders). Glue the strips around the drawing to form a frame for the picture. Leave about an inch of black paper showing around the edges.

More Ideas

❖ Research other Russian buildings that display the onion-dome style of architecture.

❖ Compare Russian architecture to architecture in other countries, such as Japan or England. Note the differences in styles of buildings constructed during the same time period.

Resources

For Teachers

A History of Russian Architecture by William Craft Brumfield (University of Washington Press, 2004). A survey of Russian architecture, from early medieval times to the present.

Landmarks of Russian Architecture: A Photographic Survey by William Craft Brumfield (Gordon & Breach, 1997). Photographs exemplify styles typical of Russian architecture.

For Students

Russia (DK Eyewitness Books) (DK, 2000). A visually appealing and fascinating introduction to various aspects of Russian history and culture, including information about architecture.

Folk Art Paintings

Students use brightly colored paints to decorate barklike paper.

The Otomi Indians of San Pablito, Mexico, descendants of the ancient Aztecs, have produced handmade paper called *amate* for many centuries. Amate is made from boiling, beating, pressing, and drying the bark of wild fig and mulberry trees. In the tradition of their ancient ancestors, indigenous people continue to use amate for sacred purposes, such as rituals performed to ensure a good harvest.

Villagers in the mountainous state of Guerrero paint on the amate, often with fluorescent acrylics. The paintings depict scenes of village life, fanciful birds, animals, and flowers. Colorful figures stand out against the unpainted brown paper backgrounds. Repeating border designs create rhythmic patterns, and variations in texture and color balance the compositions.

Getting Started

Place newspaper on the tables and prepare the work space for painting. Have students wear smocks for this project. Point out Mexico on a map and review the above information with students. Show them photographs of traditional Mexican folk art. Demonstrate the steps as students follow along.

Directions

1 Prepare the brown paper to resemble bark. Wet the paper and crumble it into a ball. Squeeze out the excess water. Open the paper and lay it flat on newspaper. Let dry.

Materials

- 10- by 12-inch brown craft paper (or brown paper bags, cut to size)
- large water containers
- newspaper
- pencils
- black permanent markers
- tempera paint in black, white, and bright or fluorescent colors (yellow, magenta, orange, turquoise, pink, red, and green)
- paintbrushes in different sizes
- 12- by 14-inch colored construction paper (optional, for mounting)

50

2 Use a pencil to draw a design inspired by nature. Encourage students to refer to the Mexican folk art samples for ideas.

3 Use a black marker to trace over the drawing.

4 Color the designs with tempera paints. Do not paint the background. The colorful designs will stand out against the brown paper background. After the paint dries, touch up lines with black marker, if needed.

Resources

For Teachers

Scholastic's Global Trek: Mexico
http://teacher.scholastic.com/
activities/globaltrek/destinations/
mexico.htm
Features information about Mexico's history and culture.

For Students

The Corn Grows Ripe by Dorothy Rhoades (Puffin, 1993). This Newbery Honor book tells the story of a Mayan boy taking over his father's responsibilities.

Latin American Arts and Cultures by Dorothy Chaplik (Davis, 2001). A survey of Latin American art from pre-Columbian times to the present.

Mexican Art and Culture by Elizabeth Lewis (Raintree, 2005). Provides an overview of the history of Mexican art.

More Ideas

❖ After the paintings are dry, mount them on sheets of construction paper in contrasting colors. Or choose paper in a color that is dominant in the design.

❖ Have students research how paper is made. You might even make paper as a class project and paint a folk art picture on it.

Carnival Masks

Students construct a carnival mask using markers, sequins, glitter, and ribbon.

The word *carnival* comes from the Italian word *carnevale*, which means "to put away the meat." Originally an Italian costume festival celebrated on the eve of Lent, Carnival traditions soon spread from Italy throughout Catholic Europe. When Europeans colonized the Americas, they brought this annual celebration with them. Africans, brought to the Americas on slave ships, also carried with them traditions for ritual and celebration, such as drumming, dancing, puppetry, and stilt-walking. Both African and Native American cultures had used feathers, bones, beads, shells, and other natural objects in the construction of headdresses, masks, and costumes for countless generations before their encounters with Europeans.

One byproduct of the European, African, and Native American cultures coming together, Carnival took on a life of its own in the Americas. Celebrations throughout the Caribbean and other parts of Latin American have developed distinct identities and traditions. Enormous costumes with spectacular headdresses, steel drum music, and wild parades are essential elements of these jubilant annual celebrations.

Getting Started

Point out the Caribbean on a map and review the above information with students. Show them photographs of masks and costumes from the Carnival celebrations in the Caribbean Islands. Demonstrate the steps as students follow along.

Materials

- photographs or samples of Caribbean carnival masks
- 9- by 12-inch tagboard or heavy construction paper (various bright colors)
- pencils
- scissors
- craft knife (optional, for adult use)
- fine-tipped markers or colored pencils
- glue
- sequins
- thin ribbon (various colors)
- small shells or beads
- glitter
- colored construction paper scraps

Directions

1 Choose a sheet of tagboard or heavy construction paper. Draw a mask outline in the shape of a face that fills the entire paper. Cut out the shape.

2 Draw eyes and, if desired, cut them out. (A teacher may need to complete this step with a craft knife.) Use a pencil to draw a mouth and nose.

3 Use markers or colored pencils to add designs to the mask. Outline the eyes and add details and designs to the other facial features. Add decoration to the cheeks and forehead. Color some areas of the designs to make them stand out.

4 Decorate the mask by gluing on sequins, ribbons, beads, shells, and paper scraps. You might cut a few feather shapes from paper and add these as well. Glitter adds a festive touch to any part of the mask.

More Ideas

❖ Play Caribbean music while students are making their masks.

❖ Make a three-dimensional mask by adding sections of cardboard with masking tape. Use papier-mâché to build up areas of the mask and to secure the cardboard sections to the mask.

Resources

For Teachers

Cajun Mardi Gras Masks by Carl Lindahl and Carolyn Ware (University Press of Mississippi, 1997). Explores the Mardi Gras celebration and its mask-making tradition through the work of six contemporary mask makers.

Caribbean Festival Arts by John W. Nunley and Judith Bettleheim (University of Washington Press, 1988). An introduction to Carnival and other Caribbean masquerade celebrations.

Paper Mask Making by Michael Grater (Dover, 1984). A guide to making various paper masks.

For Students

Under the Breadfruit Tree: Island Poems by Monica Gunning (Boyds Mills Press, 1998). More than 30 poems give a sense of Caribbean culture and life in Jamaica.

Pastel Animal Portraits

Students use pastels to depict marine animals or wildlife from the Galápagos Islands.

Six hundred miles off Ecuador's west coast, the Galápagos (guh-LAHP-uh-guhs) Islands are actually the tips of submerged, active volcanoes. Fur seals and Galápagos penguins, California sea lions and pink flamingos, giant tortoises and marine iguanas populate the Galápagos, along with a variety of insects, trees, mosses, orchids, and ferns. The plant and animal species on the islands are at the very least distinct from those on the neighboring continent, South America; some are found nowhere else on the planet. All the plants and animals found on the Galapagos first arrived on the islands by flying or swimming across the ocean or by floating on air currents. In the absence of familiar flora, natural predators, or prey, the species on the islands began a process of adapting over time to their new environment. Because each island offered different resources, species adapted differently depending on which island hosted them. Charles Darwin developed his theory of natural selection after years of studying plants and animals around the world, most famously those of the Galápagos.

Getting Started

Have students wear smocks for this project. Point out the Galápagos Islands on a map and review the above information with students. Show them photographs of marine animals and wildlife from the area. Demonstrate the steps as students follow along.

Materials

- photographs of marine animals and wildlife from the Galápagos Islands
- 10- by 16-inch dark-colored construction paper
- pencils
- white glue (in squeezable bottles)
- colored pastels
- paper towels
- 12- by 18-inch brightly colored construction paper

Directions

1. Choose an animal from the Galápagos Islands as the inspiration for your project. (The project could either be a realistic portrait of an animal or a drawing inspired by one.)

2. Use a pencil to draw the animal in the center of the 10- by 16-inch colored paper. Add large, simple details to the animals. Draw plants or scenery in the background. Overlap the elements to give the illusion of space and depth. Keep the lines of the drawing simple. (Tip: For best results, leave small areas between all lines and avoid small details.)

3. Cover the pencil lines with a thin line of glue. (When dry, the glue appears clear and the background color shows through.) Lay flat to dry.

4. Use pastels to color the spaces between the glue lines. Use the side of the chalk and avoid coloring on top of the glue lines. With a paper towel, gently blend the chalk to create the desired color or effect.

5. Mount the portrait in the center of a sheet of brightly colored construction paper.

More Ideas

❖ If desired, cut pieces from colored construction paper to resemble seaweed, plants, and so on. Cut and twist the pieces to create a textured look. Glue onto the bottom of the picture.

❖ This project also works well in conjunction with a study of barrier reefs. After studying the Great Barrier Reef in Australia or the Belize Barrier Reef, have students choose a creature to research and depict in their drawing.

Resources

For Teachers

Wildlife of the Galápagos by Julian Fitter (Princeton University Press, 2002). Features information about more than 200 species. Includes color photos.

These Web sites provide photos and information about the Galápagos:

Galápagos Conservation Trust
http://www.gct.org
Includes a section for students.

Galápagos National Park Service
http://www.galapagospark.org/png/index.php
Presents scientific and historic information about the islands.

For Students

Galápagos: Islands of Change by Lynn Born Myers and Christopher Myers (Hyperion, 1995). Color photographs accompany clear, easy-to-understand text that describes these fascinating islands and their wildlife.

Pennsylvania Dutch Barn Designs

Students paint colorful, symmetrical barn designs.

During the 17th century, many Europeans were forced to adopt a state-sanctioned religion or face persecution. Many Protestants, including Quakers, Mennonites, and Amish, immigrated to the American colonies to take advantage of William Penn's "Holy Experiment"—his design for a society characterized by religious tolerance. A diverse collection of German-speaking immigrants settled in southeastern Pennsylvania and became known as the Pennsylvania Dutch ("Dutch" is actually *Deitsch*, or "German").

These colorful Dutch "hex" designs are generally round and are painted directly on the gables of barns. Trees of life, the *distelfink* (a bird design), flowers, hearts, and six-pointed stars are popular hex signs. Colors and shapes are used symbolically: Blue indicates protection and peace; green, fertility and success; yellow, a religious connection; raindrops, crop abundance; and an oak leaf, strength. Although it is frequently said that the symbols are intended to protect people from evil, it is most likely that they are purely decorative. Consistent with the traditions of the Pennsylvania Dutch who first painted them, however, the designs remain simple and plain.

Getting Started

Place newspaper on tables and prepare the work space for painting. Have students wear smocks for this project. Point out Pennsylvania on a map and review the above information with students. Introduce them to the colors and symbols used in the designs. Distribute copies of page 59. Demonstrate the steps as students follow along.

Materials

- Pennsylvania Dutch barn designs page (page 59)
- 12- by 12-inch white drawing paper
- compasses
- rulers
- colored pencils
- erasers
- tempera paint (various colors)
- paintbrushes (various small sizes)
- scissors
- square colored construction paper (various sizes such as 11- by 11-inch, 12- by 12-inch, and 14- by 14-inch)
- glue

Directions

1 Draw several circles and sketch symmetrical designs inside them. Have students use reference books and the designs page to help them determine which symbols they would like to use.

2 Once you have selected a design, use a compass to draw a large circle on the white paper. Fill as much of the page as possible. Draw a smaller circle inside the large one. (There should be approximately 1½ inches around the smaller circle. This area will be used for a border.) Use the ruler to divide the circle into quarters.

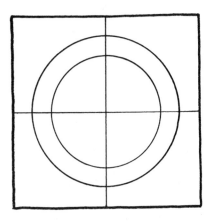

3 If you plan to have more divisions in your design, divide the circle into as many equal parts as needed.

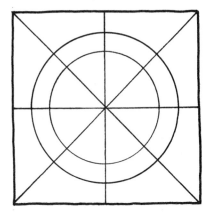

4 Draw your design inside the circle, keeping it symmetrical. Use the lines as a guide so that your design is symmetrical and has a central focal point.

Resources

For Teachers

Hex Signs: Pennsylvania Dutch Barn Symbols and Their Meanings by Don Yoder and Thomas E. Graves (Stackpole, 2000). Explores the customs and beliefs behind these traditional barn decorations. Features beautiful color photos.

5 Draw a scalloped or saw-toothed design in the border. Space the pattern as evenly as possible.

6 Determine the colors you will use in your pattern. Before you paint, lightly mark each section with a colored pencil to indicate what color paint to use. Before you paint each section, erase the mark. Carefully paint the design so that the edges are smooth and even. Let dry.

7 Cut out the circle and mount it on one or two squares of black or colored construction paper. You might position one piece of paper like a diamond and the other like a square. (See photo on page 56.)

More Ideas

❖ Invite students to work in groups to create travel brochures about Pennsylvania Dutch country. Have them include a description of the barn symbols in their brochures.

❖ While studying reference materials on the subject, note other places that these designs are used, such as on clothing, towels, and place mats. Have students design other items that feature these designs.

Traditional Pennsylvania Dutch Barn Designs

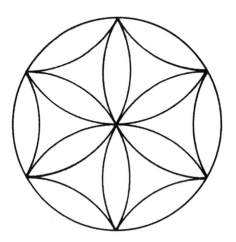

Paper Masks

Students create a paper mask in a style inspired by masks of the Tlingit.

Masks have been part of Native American ceremonies and rituals since ancient times. Northwest Coast Indian peoples, who live along the northwest coast of North America, including parts of the United States and Canada, are renowned for their elaborately carved cedar masks. Masks were traditionally made and used by different peoples of this region, including the Tlingit, Haida, Tsimshian, Bella Coola, Kwakiutl, Nootka, Makah, and Coast Salish.

Masks from this region are strikingly bold in traditional colors of red, black, green, yellow, and white. They feature ovoid shapes and S, L, and U forms, to highlight features, define outlines, and decoratively fill spaces. They are often enhanced with feathers, hair, gold, straw, and other materials. Wildlife from the region, such as the salmon, beaver, raven, whale, wolf, and bear are commonly depicted. Many masks also portray humans or mythical creatures from native legends. Three types of masks include single-faced masks carved from one piece of cedar, mechanical masks with working parts, and transformational masks with an inner and outer mask. Today, masks are still worn by trained dancers who act out stories and legends at rituals, inductions, and ceremonies.

Getting Started

On a map, point out the western shores of Canada and the northwestern coast of the United States. Review the above information with students. Show them photographs of masks and other artwork from the Northwest Coast Indian peoples. Demonstrate the steps as students follow along.

Materials

- photographs of masks from Northwest Coast Indian peoples
- sketch paper
- pencils
- 12- by 18-inch construction paper (various colors and black)
- scissors
- stapler
- 6- by 9-inch construction paper (various colors)
- glue
- tape (optional)
- raffia

Sensitivity Note
This project connects to a topic that holds deep spiritual significance for native cultures. Please impress upon your students that the project is intended to help them learn about these cultures and develop respect and appreciation for them.

Directions

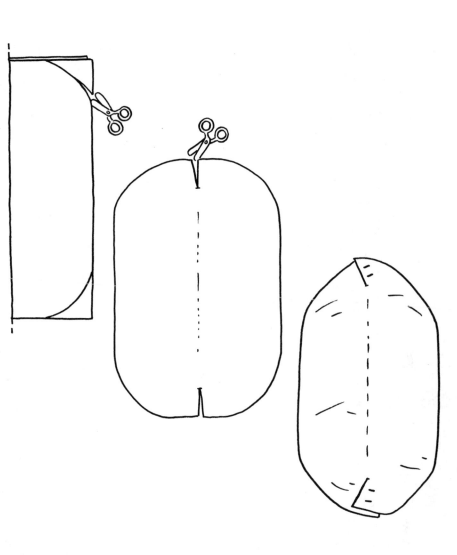

1 Draw several sketches of mask designs. Use photographs for reference as you draw.

2 After choosing a design, select a sheet of 12- by 18-inch construction paper. Fold the paper in half lengthwise. Use scissors to round the corners.

3 Cut a two-inch slit on the fold at the top of the page. Cut another two-inch slit on the fold at the bottom. Overlap the slit edges at the top and glue them together to create a three-dimensional effect. Repeat with the bottom slit edges.

4 Choose several sheets of 6- by 9-inch paper in different colors, including black. Cut a shape for the background of the eye. (Hint: To create symmetrical pieces, fold the paper and cut two of each piece.)

5 Draw and cut out an ovoid shape for the eyes. Layer smaller papers on the eye to form eyeballs.

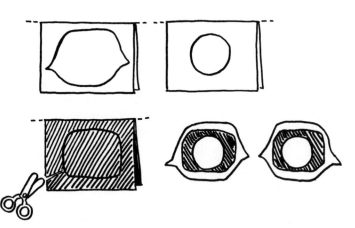

Resources

For Teachers

Learning by Designing: Pacific Northwest Coast Native Indian Art, Vol. 1 by Jim Gilbert and Karin Clark (Raven, 1999). Describes and compares four major Pacific Northwest First Nations art styles.

Learning by Designing: Pacific Northwest Coast Native Indian Art, Vol. 2 by Jim Gilbert and Karin Clark (Raven, 2002). This companion to Volume 1 delves deeper in culture and Native Indian philosophy. Includes 20 designs to draw and paint.

Seattle Art Museum
http://www.seattleartmuseum.org/
SAMcollection/code/emuseum.asp
The Native and Meso-American collection features Tlingit masks.

For Students

If You Lived With the Indians of the Northwest Coast by Anne Kamma (Scholastic, 2002). Describes daily life of several coastal peoples in a question-and-answer format.

Raven by Gerald McDermott (Harcourt Brace, 1993). This Caldecott Honor book for younger children retells the Native American tale.

6 Continue to cut shapes to cover the face with designs inspired by those of the Tlingit. Layer each part of the face with several shapes and colors of paper. Black adds contrast to the colors.

7 Fold a piece of paper in half and cut out a nose or beak shape. Glue on smaller pieces of paper to decorate it. Use glue or tape to attach the nose or beak to the mask.

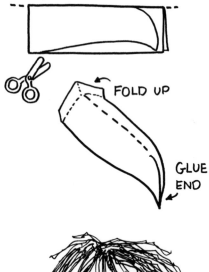

FOLD UP

GLUE END

8 Tie together small bundles of raffia. Glue or tape the bundles to the top of the mask for hair.

More Ideas

❖ Display the masks by stapling them to sheets of 12- by 18-inch black construction paper. Add cultural facts about the Northwest Coast Indian peoples to the display.

❖ Have students research the Northwest Coast Indian peoples, concentrating on the use of art throughout their culture.

:∴: **References** :∴:

Aboriginal Art of Australia: Exploring Cultural Traditions by Carol Finley (Lerner, 1999).

African Fabrics: Sewing Contemporary Fashion With Ethnic Flair by Ronke Luke-Boone (Krause, 2001).

African Masks by Iris Hahner-Herzog (Prestel, 1998).

Art From Many Hands: Multicultural Art Projects by Jo Miles Schuman (Davis, 2003).

The Art of African Masks: Exploring Cultural Traditions by Carol Finley (Lerner, 1999).

Batik by Sarah Tucker (Trafalgar Square Press, 1999).

Batik: From the Courts of Java and Sumatra by Rudolf Smend, Donald Harper, et al. (Periplus, 2004).

Brown Bag Ideas From Many Cultures by Irene Tejada (Davis, 1993).

Cajun Mardi Gras Masks by Carl Lindahl and Carolyn Ware (University Press of Mississippi, 1997).

Caribbean Festival Arts by John W. Nunley and Judith Bettleheim (University of Washington Press, 1988).

Carnival in Aruba by Victoria M. Razak (Cenda Publishing, 1998).

Castles, Codes, Calligraphy by Linda Spellman (Creative Teaching Express, 1994).

A Celtic Alphabet by Andrew Whitson (Appletree Press, 1997).

Crafts of Many Cultures by Aurelia Gomez (Scholastic, 1992).

Creative Batik by Rosi Robinson (Search Press, 2001).

Down Under: Vanishing Cultures by Jan Reynolds (Harcourt Brace, 1992).

Egyptian Hieroglyphics by Stephanie Rossini (Dover, 1989).

Egyptian Language: Easy Lessons in Egyptian Hieroglyphics by E. A. Wallis Budge (Dover, 1971).

The Egyptians by Joanna De Frates (Peter Bedrick, 2001).

Fabric (Craft Workshop) by Monica Stoppleman and Carol Crowe (Crabtree Publishing, 1998).

Greek Town by John Malam (Franklin Watts, 1999).

Hands-On Culture of West Africa by Kate O'Halloran (J. Weston Walch, 1997).

Hexology: The History and Good-Luck Meanings of the Hex Symbols by Jacob Zook (Jacob Zook, 1990).

Hex Signs: Pennsylvania Dutch Barn Symbols and Their Meanings by Don Yoder and Thomas E. Graves (Stackpole, 2000).

Hieroglyphics: The Writing of Ancient Egypt by Norma Jean Katan (Atheneum, 1981).

A History of Russian Architecture by William Craft Brumfield (University of Washington Press, 2004).

Hmong Textile Designs by Anthony Chong (Stemmer House, 1990).

The Illuminated Alphabet by Timothy Noad and Patricia Seligman (Sterling, 1994).

Latin American Arts and Cultures by Dorothy Chaplik (Davis, 2001).

Learning by Designing: Pacific Northwest Coast Native Indian Art, Vol. 1 by Jim Gilbert and Karin Clark (Raven, 1999).

Learning by Designing: Pacific Northwest Coast Native Indian Art, Vol. 2 by Jim Gilbert and Karin Clark (Raven, 2002).

Look What Came From Greece by Kevin Davis (Franklin Watts, 1999).

Masks of Black Africa by Ladislas Segy (Dover, 1975).

Northwest Coast Indian Art: An Analysis of Form by Bill Holm (University of Washington Press, 1965).

Northwest Coast Indian Designs by Madeleine Orban-Szontagh (Dover, 1994).

Northwest Indian Designs by Caren Caraway (Stemmer House, 1982).

Paper (Craft Workshop) by Helen Bliss (Crabtree, 1998).

Paper Mask Making by Michael Grater (Dover, 1984).

The Royal Arts of Africa: The Majesty of Forms by Suzanne Preston Blier (Harry N. Abrams, 1998).

Sea and Cedar: How the Northwest Coast Indians Lived by Lois McConkey (Madrona, 1973).

Serengeti: Natural Order on the African Plain by Mitsuaki Iwago (Chronicle Books, 1987).

Teaching With Folk Stories of the Hmong: An Activity Book by Dia Cha and Norma Livo (Libraries Unlimited, 2000).

Understanding Northwest Coast Art: A Guide to Crests, Beings, and Symbols by Cheryl Shearar (University of Washington Press, 2000).

What Do We Know About Greeks? by Anne Pearson (Franklin Watts, 1992).